Wild Predators!

Killer Carnivores

Heinemann
LIBRARY

Andrew Solway

www.heinemann.co.uk/library
Visit our website to find out more information about **Heinemann Library** books.

To order:
 Phone 44 (0) 1865 888066
Send a fax to 44 (0) 1865 314091
Visit the Heinemann Bookshop at www.heinemann.co.uk/library to browse our catalogue and order online.

First published in Great Britain by
Heinemann Library, Halley Court, Jordan Hill,
Oxford OX2 8EJ, part of Harcourt Education.
Heinemann is a registered trademark of Harcourt
Education Ltd.

Editorial: Nancy Dickmann, Tanvi Rai and Sarah
Chappelow
Design: David Poole and Calcium
Illustrations: Geoff Ward
Picture Research: Maria Joannou and Catherine
Bevan
Production: Camilla Smith

Originated by Ambassador Litho Ltd.
Printed and bound in China by
South China Printing Company.
The paper used to print this book comes from
sustainable resources.

ISBN 0 431 19005 4
08 07 06 05
10 9 8 7 6 5 4 3 2 1

**British Library Cataloguing in Publication
Data**
Solway, Andrew
Killer Carnivores. – (Wild predators)
 599.7'73153
A full catalogue record for this book is available
from the British Library.

Acknowledgements
The Publishers would like to thank the following
for permission to reproduce photographs:
Ardea pp. **6** (M Watson), **11** (M Watson), **19**
(James Marchington), **22** (Kenneth W Fink), **27
top** (Tom & Pat Leeson), **28** (M Watson), **35
bottom** (Clem Haagner), **41 bottom** (Clem
Haagner); Corbis pp. **7 top, 8, 9 top, 9 bottom**
(Dan Guravich), **12** (Galen Rowell), **15 top** (Chris
Knights), **15 bottom** (Ian Beames), **24** (S.
Charlie Brown), **39** (Gallo Images), **40**; FLPA pp.
4 (Minden Pictures), **5 top** (Wendy Dennis), **5
bottom** (Derek Middleton), **13** (Minden Pictures),
16 (S & D & K Maslowski), **18** (Michael Clark),
21 (Mikhail Zhilin), **23** (E & D Hosking), **26**
(Mark Newman), **30** (Gerard Lacz), **35 top** (F
Hartmann), **36** (Minden Pictures), **41 top**
(D Zingel Eichhom), **43** (Hugh Clark); NHPA pp.
10 (Bryan & Cherry Alexander), **14** (Stephen
Krasemann), **31 top** (Kitchin & B Hurst), **31
bottom** (Bill Coster), **32** (Daniel Heuclin), **34**
(Nigel J Dennis), **38** (Jonathan & Angela Scott),
42 (Dave Watts); Oxford Scientific Films pp. **17**
(Richard Kolar), **20** (Tom Ulrich), **25** (Doug Allan),
27 bottom (Berndt Fischer), **33** (Mark Deeble &
Victoria Stone), **37** (Mark Powles); Photodisc p.
7 bottom.

Cover photograph of brown bear catching
Salmon, Brook Falls, Katmai National Park,
Alaska reproduced with permission of
Steve Bloom.

The Publishers would like to thank Michael Bright
of the BBC Natural History Unit for his
assistance in the preparation of this book.

Every effort has been made to contact copyright
holders of any material reproduced in this book.
Any omissions will be rectified in subsequent
printings if notice is given to the Publishers.

Contents

Any words appearing in the text in bold, **like this**, are explained in the Glossary.

Carnivores

Carnivores are animals that eat other animals. Many different kinds of animals are carnivores, from spiders and dragonflies to sharks. Among the **mammals**, many species of land-living carnivores belong to an **order** (group) of mammals called the Carnivora – Carnivores with a capital C.

Today's Carnivores are descended from ancestors called miacids that lived 60 million years ago. Modern Carnivores range from the tiny 15-centimetre (6-inch) least weasel to the huge 2.5-metre (8-foot) polar bear.

Carnivore families

Most zoologists divide the Carnivores into eight different subgroups, known as **families**. They are cats, dogs, bears, **mustelids** (weasels and their relatives), procyonids (raccoons and kinkajous), hyenas, mongooses, and civets (small, cat-like animals). Cats and dogs are dealt with in other books in this series.

Carnivore families can be broadly divided into a cat branch and a dog branch. Most members of the cat branch have retractable claws that are kept sharp for use as weapons, while most members of the dog group have thicker, blunt claws used for grip and for digging. As well as the cat family, the cat branch includes hyenas, mongooses, and civets, while the dog branch includes bears and mustelids.

Not all members of the Carnivore order hunt animals for food. Some are **omnivores**, eating a mixture of plant and animal food, and at least one (the giant panda) eats mainly plants. But many Carnivores are deadly **predators**.

At the back of its mouth a Carnivore has a set of teeth called the carnassials. The sharp edges of these teeth slide past each other like a pair of scissors, to slice through meat.

Easy eating, hard to catch

Animals that eat plants must eat almost continuously to get enough nutrients from their food. Meat is very nutritious, so predators can manage on one good meal every few days.

When it comes to finding and catching food, however, it is another matter. Animals do not stay in one place and wait to be eaten. They run and hide, and if they are cornered they will often lash out. A predator needs good senses to find prey, and must be fast and agile to catch it. Finally, predators need weapons, such as sharp teeth and claws, to kill prey quickly and avoid injury.

Mongooses (like this one) and meerkats belong to the cat branch of carnivores.

Pouched predators

Not all mammalian predators are Carnivores. One group of predators are more closely related to kangaroos than to cats. These are the **marsupial** predators, found in Australia and the Americas.

Millions of years in the past, there were many marsupial predators in Australia. They included killer kangaroos and a marsupial lion. Today, only a few marsupial predators survive. The largest and best known of them is the Tasmanian devil.

The mustelid family includes weasels, stoats (shown here), badgers, otters, and minks. Nearly all mustelids are fierce predators.

Polar bear

There is nothing to see except new-fallen snow, but the polar bear can smell that a seal has been here recently. Occasionally the bear stands up on its well-furred feet, but most of the time it lies motionless. If it moves or makes a sound, the seal will not come back to its breathing hole. After hours of patient waiting, the polar bear is rewarded – a seal comes up to breathe. The bear explodes into action, leaping forward and smashing its huge paw down on the seal's skull.

Polar bears are some of the biggest **predators** on land. The largest bears can be 2.5 metres (8 feet) long and weigh over 600 kilograms (1322 pounds). Polar bears spend most of their lives on the pack ice that covers the Arctic Ocean.

Pack ice

The surface of the Arctic Ocean is a giant ice sheet. Pack ice is ice that is not connected to land. It is not one continuous, flat sheet. In some places the ice forms ridges 30 metres (98 feet) high. In other places there are areas of open water, called leads. The pack ice moves slowly around the North Pole.

Polar bears have black skin, to absorb any heat from the sun. You can see the blackness around the nose. Their fur is actually colourless, but it appears white.

Polar bears are fast and agile for their size. They can run at over 56 km/h (35 mph), and can fight standing on the back legs.

At home in the cold

Polar bears can survive in the harsh conditions of the Arctic all year round, both on the ice and in the freezing Arctic waters. Like most **mammals**, polar bears have a coat of fur to help keep them warm. But the fur of brown bears, which live in warmer areas, is thicker than a polar bear's fur. This is because a polar bear does not rely on its fur alone to keep it warm. Like seals and whales, it has a thick layer of fat (blubber) beneath the skin that helps keep it warm. This fat layer is particularly important in water, because a polar bear's fur is not a good **insulator** when it is wet.

The polar bear has plenty of insulation to keep it warm, but the way it behaves also helps it to survive in harsh conditions. In an Arctic blizzard, freezing cold winds can make even a polar bear lose heat. In this kind of weather, bears protect themselves by digging a hollow in the snow to get out of the wind. In the Arctic winter, females that are pregnant with cubs dig themselves a den and **hibernate**. Male polar bears and females that are not pregnant also dig dens in severe weather.

Polar bears are at home in the water. They can swim for many kilometres, using their broad front paws to paddle.

Finding prey

A polar bear's main prey is seals. Like polar bears, seals are mammals, and must breathe regularly to survive. They do this by keeping open small holes in the ice where they can surface to breathe. Polar bears look for these breathing holes because they are good spots to find seals.

Finding small breathing holes among the vast, jumbled wastes of the Arctic ice sheet might seem an impossible task. But polar bears have excellent senses to help them. They have good hearing, and their night vision is better than ours. A polar bear's most remarkable sense organ is its nose. Its sense of smell is even better than that of a dog or a wolf. It can scent **prey** from a distance of several kilometres (1–2 miles), if the wind is in the right direction. More often than not, a polar bear finds prey by following its nose.

Hunting on the ice

A polar bear's favourite hunting ground is on the thick sheet of pack ice that floats on the surface of the Arctic Ocean. Most often it will hunt seals by ambushing them at their breathing holes. When a seal comes up to breathe, a polar bear must make a lightning attack, or the seal will dive and escape. Once the seal is dead, the polar bear grabs it in its mouth and hauls the seal from the water.

Polar bears have tremendous strength in their neck and shoulders.

Polar bears generally catch ringed seals at breathing holes. A ringed seal (the polar bear's usual food) weighs about 90 kilograms (200 pounds). To get it out of the water, the polar bear must haul it through a breathing hole that is usually quite small – far smaller than the seal's body. But the polar bear is so strong that it can break the ice to pull the seal through the small breathing hole.

As the ice freezes in winter, belugas (white whales) sometimes get trapped at ice holes far from open water. These whales are over 4 metres (13 feet) long, but they are not safe from polar bears.

Spring feast

Spring is an important hunting time for polar bears. At this time ringed seal mothers give birth to their cubs in dens dug in the ice. These dens may have several feet of packed snow above them. However, a polar bear's nose can pick up the scent of a seal cub in its den even through the snow. Once a bear finds the location of a seal den, it crashes down, front feet first, on top of the den to cave in the roof and get at the seal cub inside.

Arctic foxes often follow polar bears and **scavenge** their kills.

Hungry in summer

In summer, the southern edges of the pack ice melt, and most polar bears follow the ice edge. Other bears become stranded on islands, where it is hard to get enough food. Some bears move on to the mainland, but they find it difficult to survive because they cannot hunt seals. They must live on small prey, such as ground squirrels. They also eat roots, berries, and kelp (a kind of seaweed), and **scavenge** food.

In summer, polar bears may wander into human settlements looking for food. They may scavenge on rubbish dumps (as seen in this picture) or break into food stores.

Born in the winter

Polar bears **mate** in the spring, but the young do not begin to develop in the female's **womb** until autumn. Once the babies do start to develop, the female digs herself a den in the snow on land, where she will spend the winter.

Bear cubs are born in November and December in the den that the female has dug. From then until March the mother and her cubs stay inside the den. The mother does not eat or drink, and all through the winter she feeds her cubs on her milk.

By spring the cubs are well developed and able to follow the mother when she leaves the den. This is the time when seals are producing cubs, and the seal cubs provide enough food to feed mother polar bears and their cubs.

The cubs stay with their mother for about 30 months, by which time they can hunt successfully for themselves. They may live for 20 years or more.

Amazing hibernators

Female polar bears may go without food for as long as eight months, and all polar bears hibernate in shelters for weeks on end when the weather is bad. To survive in these conditions, the bears store up large amounts of fat when food is abundant. The bears can then live on their fat stores, neither eating or drinking, for weeks or months.

When polar bears hibernate, it is very different from hibernation in small animals, such as squirrels and mice. When small animals hibernate, their body temperature falls very low, and they wake up only slowly. Every few days they need to drink and get rid of wastes. When polar bears hibernate they can wake easily. Their body temperature remains almost normal (although their heart rate slows down), and they do not produce wastes or need to drink.

At birth in early winter, a polar bear cub weighs just 600 grams (21 ounces), but by spring it weighs 10 to 15 kilograms (22 to 33 pounds). The only food it gets during this period is its mother's milk.

Brown bear

In Yellowstone Park, USA, a female grizzly and her young cub are attacked by a wolf pack. The wolves hope to distract the mother and snatch the cub. Again and again they rush at the female and she lunges angrily at them. There are several near misses – the bear is surprisingly fast for her size. After a few minutes the wolves decide the hunt is too risky. One blow from the bear could break a wolf's back. They trot away, leaving the bears in peace.

Grizzly bears, Kodiak bears, Kamchatka bears – these are all names for types of brown bear. Brown bears are the most widespread of all bears. They live in northern parts of the world in a range of different **habitats**. They also live in parts of Europe and the Middle East. They range in size from about 150 centimetres (60 inches) long in Europe, to 280 centimetres (9 feet) in Alaska and eastern Russia.

Not just meat

Brown bears are not just meat-eaters; they are **omnivores**. The word omnivore means "eat everything" – and brown bears certainly do! They eat large amounts of berries and nuts, and they dig up roots, insects, and burrowing mammals. When salmon swim upstream to their **spawning** grounds, brown bears fish in the rapids and waterfalls. And in late spring, when deer and elk have their calves, brown bears go hunting.

The biggest brown bears can stand three metres (about ten feet) tall on their hind legs.

When they choose to hunt, brown bears are fierce predators. They have good hearing and an excellent sense of smell. Their dagger-like **canine** teeth and long, heavy claws are formidable weapons. They can run at speeds of almost 50 km/h (about 30 mph), twice as fast as the average human. Although young deer and elk are good runners, they are not quick enough to escape from an adult brown bear.

Surviving the winter

In the winter across the northern parts of the brown bear's range, there is not enough food to keep a large animal going. The bears get around this problem by hibernating. Like polar bears, brown bears do not need to eat or drink for months when they hibernate. Before hibernating, the bears build up large reserves of fat, which are used up during their winter **fast**.

In early spring each year, thousands of Pacific salmon swim up the rivers of Alaska to **mate** and lay their eggs. Large numbers of brown bears gather to feast on the salmon.

Females give birth to cubs during their time in their winter dens. The cubs are really tiny when they are first born – each weighs less than a kilogram (under two pounds). They are born during the winter because this gives them the maximum amount of time to build up fat reserves before the following winter, when they too will have to hibernate.

Weasel, stoat, mink, and polecat

On a grassy slope in England, a stoat steals up on a group of feeding rabbits. When it is close, the stoat does something amazing. It bursts out and begins to leap around, somersaulting and chasing its tail in a frenzied "dance". Most of the rabbits scatter, but the one closest to the stoat stares, mesmerised. With one more bound, the stoat leaps on the staring rabbit and bites the back of its neck.

There are many stories of stoats and weasels "dancing" like this. There is no doubt that it happens, although some scientists think that the dancing is caused by a disease the animals get.

Stoats and weasels are **mustelids** – the largest and most varied Carnivore family. The mustelids get their name from a pouch under the tail that produces a sticky, smelly liquid called musk. Musk is used for **scent marking** and sometimes as a defence against larger **predators**. Mustelids range in size from the least weasel, which can be less than 20 centimetres (about 8 inches) from head to tail, to the sea otter, which can be 6 times longer and weigh 1000 times more.

The American mink was introduced to Europe during the 1920s. Since then it has taken over in many areas from the European mink.

In northern areas, stoats and least weasels grow a white coat in winter. White stoats, or ermines, are farmed for their fur.

Small mustelids

Stoats and weasels are two of a closely related group (**genus**) of sixteen small mustelids. All of them are long-bodied predators that between them hunt just about every kind of prey animal up to the size of rabbits. Of the small mustelids, the best-studied species are least and long-tailed weasels, stoats, European and steppe polecats, and American and European minks.

Least weasels are common around the world from the Arctic in the north to northern Africa in the south. Stoats and American minks are almost as widespread. Long-tailed weasels live in much of North America and northern South America. European minks and polecats are found only in Europe, and steppe polecats live in the **steppes** and semi-deserts of Russia.

Between them, small mustelids live in almost every possible **habitat**. Least weasels are found in almost any habitat where there is good ground cover. They have also adapted to living in towns. Stoats and long-tailed weasels live in similar habitats, but are also found in more open country. Minks are found close to rivers or lakes. European polecats live in woods and forests, parkland, marshes, and along coasts.

Polecats can be recognized by the light and dark "mask" markings on their face.

Sizes and prey

The least weasel is smallest of the mustelids. Stoats are generally bigger and heavier, while long-tailed weasels are bigger still, but there is some overlap in size between the different species. In all species, males are bigger than females. Minks and polecats are bigger than weasels and stoats. They range from 32 to 56 centimetres (about 12 to 22 inches) in length, not counting the tail.

Weasels and stoats hunt mainly **rodents** and rabbits. Least weasels concentrate on mice and voles, while stoats and long-tailed weasels usually catch larger prey, such as rats and rabbits. Rabbits are also a polecat's main prey.

Small mustelids must hunt constantly to get enough food. Their thin bodies lose heat rapidly, so they must burn lots of energy simply to keep warm. This weasel is eating a meadow mouse.

Too specialized to survive

Most small mustelids have a few main types of prey, but the black-footed ferret (a kind of polecat) specialized in hunting only one species – the prairie dog. Until the 19th century there were millions of prairie dogs on the North American plains, but then farmers, who saw them as pests, killed off huge numbers. The black-footed ferret lost its major food source, and became extinct in the wild. However, some ferrets were bred in captivity and in recent years some captive ferrets have been reintroduced into the wild.

Minks hunt a much wider range of prey. They live near to water, so they often hunt fish, frogs, and crayfish. But they also catch prey on land, including mice, voles, muskrats, rabbits, and birds.

Small but deadly

Despite their size, small mustelids are deadly hunters. A stoat, for instance, can kill a rabbit almost ten times its own weight.

Small mustelids hunt mainly on or below the ground. Their long, slim bodies allow them to follow prey animals down their burrows. Least weasels hunt underground most often, chasing mice and voles through their burrows and runs. In winter, both least weasels and stoats hunt lemmings along tunnels that the lemmings dig under the snow.

A killing bite

Small mustelids are very efficient killers. When a stoat bites the back of a rabbit's neck, the rabbit is killed almost instantly. This deadly accuracy is very important for such small predators. If a weasel or stoat fluffs its first attack, it can easily be injured or killed as its prey lashes out in panic.

Sometimes a neck bite is not the best way to kill prey, so small mustelids will use other techniques. For instance, polecats will kill small prey with a chest bite. If an animal turns to defend itself, they then go for its throat, rather than the back of the neck.

Since 1991, groups of black-footed ferrets bred in captivity have been released into the wild each year. Scientists hope to have a population of 1500 ferrets in the wild by 2010.

Living alone

Small mustelids are solitary hunters, and they also live alone. Each animal has its own **territory** – the area where it lives and hunts. The territories of male and female weasels overlap, but a male will not tolerate another male in his territory, and females do not tolerate other females. Both sexes mark their territory with scent from their musk pouches.

Within its territory, a small mustelid will have several dens where it can rest, eat, and hide from larger predators. These dens are often burrows taken over from their prey. In winter, northern stoats and weasels keep their burrows warm and cosy by lining them with the fur of their victims.

Early spring is a time when many small mustelids **mate**. At this time of year, males may leave their territories to go looking for females. Both males and females mate several times, with more than one partner.

The race to breed

A least weasel is unlikely to live for more than a year or two. Stoats live only two years, while other species live up to four or five years. All these species try to produce as many offspring as possible in their short lives.

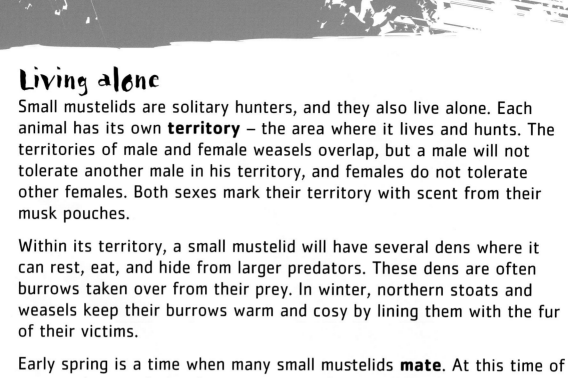

A polecat litter is born in a straw nest. In colder areas the nest chamber is fur-lined.

Polecat pets

Ferrets are domesticated polecats that have been bred to hunt for rabbits. The ancient Greeks mention using ferrets for hunting over 2400 years ago. Today hunting with ferrets is banned in some countries. In other countries ferrets are still used for hunting, and everywhere they are kept as pets.

Weasels' lives are short, but they grow and develop quickly, so a female can produce two **litters** in one year. Up to eight cubs are born in one litter, about 5 weeks after mating. The cubs have little hair at birth and their eyes are closed. For three weeks the cubs feed only on their mother's milk, then they begin to eat meat. By six or seven weeks old, the weasels are beginning to hunt, and for a short time they hunt as a group with their mother. Between nine and twelve weeks they leave their mother, and are ready to mate for themselves.

Larger weasels, minks, and polecats breed only once a year, but they also develop quickly, and are hunting for themselves by the age of twelve weeks.

When hunting rabbits, a ferret is put down one hole in a warren, and nets are spread over the other holes. The ferret drives the rabbits out of the warren and into the nets.

Marten and fisher

An American marten sails from the branches of one tree into another, tail lashing for balance. It runs along a branch and then stops, frozen. It has heard the cheeping of nestlings in the tree above. But a group of birds have seen the marten, and they mob it, flying around and calling loudly. The marten remains still until one bird comes too close. Then it leaps and strikes, and the bird falls in a flurry of feathers.

Martens are a group of medium-sized **mustelids**, most of which live in forests and are agile climbers. The American marten (the smallest) is similar in size to a polecat, while the fisher (the largest marten) is 47 to 75 centimetres (18 to 30 inches) long, not counting its tail, and weighs 2 to 5 kilograms (4 to 11 pounds). Like small mustelids, martens have a long body, but their legs are longer, and they have a bushy tail.

From forests to towns

There are eight species of marten and fisher. The pine marten, the sable, the Japanese marten, and the American marten are all very similar animals that live mainly in forests in Europe, northern Asia, Japan, and North America. The yellow-throated marten and the Nilgiri marten live in forests further south, in south-east Asia, southern Russia, and southern India. The stone marten prefers more open country, including rocky areas. It is also found close to towns and cities. The fisher lives in dense forest areas in North America.

Pine martens are well adapted for life in trees. Their long, bushy tail helps them balance, and their large feet have hairs between the pads to help them grip.

Hunted for fur

Like the smaller minks and ermines, many martens have been hunted for their fur for hundreds of years. The thick, dark, glossy fur of the sable, found in northern Asia, is the most valuable marten fur. By the 18th century, hundreds of thousands of sables were being killed for their fur each year. By the early 20th century, they had disappeared from large parts of their range.

During the later 20th century, sables were protected, and their numbers climbed rapidly. Today about 250,000 wild sables and 27,000 sables raised on fur farms are killed each year for their fur.

A varied diet

Martens eat a much wider range of food than small mustelids. Mice, squirrels, other small mammals, birds, eggs, and insects are all on a marten's menu. They also eat berries, fruits, and honey. Although they are very agile in trees, they do much of their hunting on the ground. Despite their name, fish is not an important item on the fisher's menu. It prefers to eat other **prey**, such as porcupines.

Only the thick, glossy winter coat of a sable is valuable as fur. In the summer, its coat is dull and thin.

Larger prey

Two kinds of marten hunt larger prey. In the foothills of the Himalayas, yellow-throated martens hunt musk deer and the young of other hoofed mammals. In the forests of Canada and the northern USA, fishers hunt a really tough customer – the North American porcupine.

Hunting porcupines

North American porcupines are large, heavy animals – a big male can be 90 centimetres (3 feet) long and weigh 12 kilograms (26 pounds). A porcupine may be slow-moving, but it is no pushover as prey because its body is covered in long, barbed quills that could give a **predator** a painful injury. Even large predators, such as lynxes and coyotes, are wary of porcupines.

When a porcupine is threatened, it turns its back on its enemy, presenting a mass of long quills. The fisher circles the porcupine, trying to get round to the head, which is not covered in quills. It makes lightning attacks to bite the porcupine's face. Eventually the fisher may get in a good attack and disable the porcupine, or slow it down. Then it flips the porcupine over, and attacks its unprotected belly.

Although porcupines are dangerous and difficult prey, for a fisher they are worth the effort. A single porcupine can provide food for a fisher for anything from ten days to a month.

Fishers are larger than other martens, and less agile. Other martens have a patch of lighter fur on the throat, but fishers do not have this.

Raising young

Like small mustelids, martens live and hunt alone, except when males and females meet to **mate**. Most marten cubs are born in the late spring, in a small cave or a hollow log, or even in the old nest of a crow or magpie.

Most litters have three or four cubs, but there can be up to eight young. The cubs' eyes do not open until about five weeks old – in fishers not until they are seven weeks. Marten cubs feed on their mother's milk until they are six to ten weeks old, and are independent after four or five months.

Delayed development

Most martens mate in the summer, but marten cubs are not born until the spring of the following year. This is not because the cubs take a long time to grow in the mother's womb, but because their development is delayed. Delaying the cubs' birth until spring means that the cubs grow up during spring and summer, when there is plenty of food, so they have the best chance of surviving the winter.

Otters

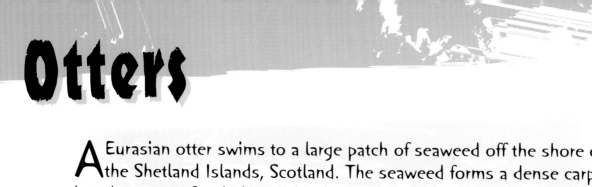

A Eurasian otter swims to a large patch of seaweed off the shore of the Shetland Islands, Scotland. The seaweed forms a dense carpet, but there are a few holes. Going in through one of these holes, the otter begins to search for fish hiding among the seaweed. After a few short dives, it snatches its first fish and brings it to the surface to eat.

Otters are the only group of **mustelids** that have really taken to the water. There are about thirteen different otter species around the world. The most widespread species is the Eurasian otter, which is found by rivers and lakes (and sometimes on the coast) across much of Europe and Asia. The hairy-nosed otter is a similar species found in South-east Asia, while northern, southern, and neotropical river otters live in similar habitats in North and South America.

Eurasian otters died out in many areas because of over-hunting and river pollution. However in some places hunting bans and river cleanups have increased their numbers.

When moving slowly in water, an otter uses its webbed front paws, but to move quickly its uses its large hind flippers and steers with its tail.

Sharp senses

Otters look similar to weasels and other mustelid relatives, but they are adapted to living and hunting in water.

Like other mustelids, otters have sharp senses. Underwater, their nose and ears close to stop water entering, so they must rely on sight and touch. Otters can see almost as well underwater as they can on land. Vision is important for hunting in clear water by day, but at night touch and vibration are more important. Otters have long whiskers on their snouts and on their elbows. These stiff hairs are sensitive to touch and to vibrations caused by the movements of **prey**.

Keeping warm

One problem for otters is how to keep warm in water. Animals swimming in water lose heat 25 times faster than they do on land. Unlike polar bears, otters do not have a layer of fatty blubber to help them keep warm in the water. All they have is their fur, which is especially fine and dense. Sea otters have the densest fur of all.

Tool users

Sea otters are among the few animals that use tools. Shellfish, such as clams and abalones, are sea otters' favourite foods. To break open their shells, a sea otter floats on its back with a flat stone on its chest and smashes the shellfish against the stone.

Fish-eaters and clam-diggers

There are broadly two types of feeders among the otters. Some species, such as the short-clawed otters, have sensitive front paws that they use for feeling along the riverbed or raking through the mud for crabs and shellfish. The sea otter also hunts for shellfish, but in the sea rather than in fresh water.

Other otter species hunt fish and other more active prey. These otters catch their prey by chasing them and grabbing them with their sharp teeth rather than searching with their front paws.

When hunting, otters make short dives of less than a minute. They eat the smaller fish they catch at the surface, but they carry larger and more awkward prey to land. Eurasian otters eat mainly eels and fish about 30 centimetres (12 inches) long or smaller. Giant otters, northern river otters, and smooth otters catch larger fish, and northern river otters occasionally kill muskrats and beavers.

Eurasian otters live and hunt alone, but many otters are more sociable. Smooth otters and short-clawed otters, for instance, live in small groups, while male North American river otters sometimes live in slightly larger "bachelor groups". Sea otters are the most sociable otters. The females and their young live together in "rafts" of up to 40 otters, while in winter male sea otters gather in groups of up to 150. Smaller groups work together when hunting prey.

When they are not busy hunting or diving, otters like to relax by floating on their backs.

Other otters spend some time on land, but a sea otter spends its whole life in the water. In this picture it is using a stone to crack open a clam.

Raising young

Most otters give birth to between one and five cubs, nine or ten weeks after **mating**. In more sociable otters both parents help with the young, but female Eurasian river otters bring up their young alone. Young otters are very playful. They roll and tumble on shore, chase each other in the water, and make mud slides on river banks. As with many carnivores, the mother teaches her young to hunt by catching prey, then releasing them still alive for the young to try and catch.

Trained to fish

Short-clawed otters in the wild eat snails and shellfish, but fishermen in South-east Asia have taught them to fish. The otters are released into the water wearing harnesses, and chase shoals of fish into the fishermen's nets. They are allowed to keep any fish they catch.

The giant otter is the longest of the otters, but the sea otter is heavier. Giant otters, like the family seen resting in this picture, live across much of South America.

American badger

On the North American plains, a badger has caught the scent of ground squirrels. It follows the trail to a hole underneath some bushes. Sniffing around, the badger finds several more holes. It blocks up all the openings except one. Then it begins to dig furiously at the final hole, in a race to reach the ground squirrels before they dig themselves out.

Badgers are a very different shape from long-bodied **mustelids**, such as weasels and otters, although they are related. These stocky, powerful animals have spade-like front legs that are built for digging.

American badgers live in North America, from western Canada, south to Mexico. Their main habitat is prairie grassland. Badger species in other parts of the world are **omnivores**, but the American badger is a fierce **predator**.

Underground hunters

The main **prey** of American badgers are small burrowing animals, especially ground squirrels and prairie dogs. They use their sensitive noses and sharp hearing to locate prey, then dig down to catch them. Their powerful jaws and sharp **canines** make short work of any animal they catch.

All badgers have striking black and white markings on their face. The markings may warn enemies that badgers are tough customers.

American badgers can dig at tremendous speed – on one occasion three people digging with shovels were unable to catch up with an American badger digging a tunnel.

Sitting out the winter

In the northern parts of the American badger's range, there is little food to be found during the winter. Badgers spend much of the cold weather resting in underground dens. Although the badgers may sleep for several days at a stretch if the weather is bad, they do not truly **hibernate**.

Like martens, badgers mate in the summer but the cubs are not born until the following spring. Development of the cubs is delayed until the end of winter, so that the cubs have the whole of the spring and summer to grow and develop before their first winter.

Growing up

American badgers produce one to five cubs. At birth they weigh less than 100 grams (3.5 ounces), and their eyes are closed. Their eyes do not open until the cubs are about a month old. They stay with their mother until the autumn, when the family splits up.

Although coyotes clearly benefit from pairing up with American badgers, it is not clear what the benefit is to the badgers.

Hunting partners

American badgers sometimes team up to hunt with coyotes. The badger finds the burrow of a group of prey animals, and digs down to find them. Any prey that escapes from the burrow is picked off by the coyote above ground.

Wolverine

In the conifer forests of Siberia the snow lies in thick drifts. A reindeer comes plunging through the trees, sinking into the snow with each step. Behind the reindeer is what looks like a small, chocolate brown bear. Its large, furry feet carry it over the snowdrifts with ease. It quickly catches up with the reindeer and leaps on its back. The reindeer has no time to struggle before the animal's sharp teeth are buried deep in its neck.

Wolverines are little bigger than Springer spaniels, but they are powerful and ferocious hunters. They live in conifer forests, mountains, and icy **tundra** in the north of Europe, Russia and North America.

Winter feeding

Wolverines will hunt anything they can catch, but in winter they kill more large **prey**, such as reindeer (caribou) or other deer. Their snowshoe-like feet give them an advantage when running in deep snow. The large, flat shape spreads the weight so they don't sink into the snow.

Carrion is also an important food source, especially in winter. A wolverine's strong jaws and teeth can tear up large carcasses and crunch open bones.

Pretty strong!

A wolverine is immensely strong for its size. If wolverines were the size of bears, they would be the strongest animals in the world.

Although they look like short-legged bears, wolverines are mustelids. They have an excellent sense of smell, and their strong jaws can even crunch up bones.

A wolverine can kill a caribou many times larger than itself. Wolverines are sometimes called gluttons, because they can eat a huge amount in one sitting.

Tougher in summer

In summer wolverines lose the speed advantage that their large paws give them on snow. They hunt smaller prey, such as rodents, rabbits, and hares, and slower animals, such as porcupines. Like fishers, wolverines have learned to avoid a porcupine's quills. In autumn, wolverines may add fruit and berries to their diet.

Thinly spread

In the areas where wolverines live, prey animals are few and far between. Wolverines have to be very thinly spread to find enough food. They live and hunt alone, except for a brief time in the summer when males and females meet up and **mate**.

As with some other **mustelids**, the cubs do not begin to develop straight after mating. They begin to grow in the mother's **womb** in January or February, and are born in March or April.

Dens and birth

Shortly before giving birth, female wolverines dig a den under the snow. The cubs are born with a coat of white fur. They stay in or close to the den for about six weeks, after which they begin to travel with their mother on hunting trips. After about ten weeks they start to eat meat. Young wolverines stay with their mother until the beginning of winter, when the family splits up.

Wolverines often steal the kills of larger predators such as wolves. They are completely unafraid, and have a truly ferocious growl.

Mongooses

The cobra rears up, hissing in anger. It draws back and tries to strike, but the mongoose is too quick for it. The mongoose dances round the cobra, rocking and swaying, its tail fluffed up like a cat's. The cobra strikes again and again, but always too late. Eventually the snake begins to tire, and then the fight is almost over. With a final leap, the mongoose grabs the back of the cobra's neck and bites down hard.

Mongooses are best known for killing snakes, but not all of them are snake-hunters. There are about 35 different species of mongoose. These small, long-bodied animals look similar to weasels and stoats, but they are a separate Carnivore family. They live in warm parts of the world, from Spain and Africa east to China and Indonesia. Mongooses survive in a variety of habitats, from forests to deserts.

Snake-Killers

In a story in Rudyard Kipling's *Jungle Book*, the mongoose Rikki-Tikki-Tavi kills Nag and Nagaina, two king cobras. Rikki-Tikki-Tavi was an Indian Grey mongoose, but two other species, the Javan and Egyptian mongooses, are especially known for hunting snakes.

One story in Rudyard Kipling's Jungle Book, is about Rikki-Tikki-Tavi, a mongoose that kills two king cobras. This is not just fiction. Indian Grey mongooses really are capable of killing such deadly snakes.

For all these mongooses, snakes are only a small part of their diet. With their lightning speed and tremendous agility, they make short work of small **prey**, such as mice, lizards, and insects. Egyptian mongooses also hunt larger animals, such as rabbits and even other mongooses. Eggs and sometimes fruit are also on the mongoose menu.

Several other mongoose species also hunt mainly small mammals. Slender mongooses, for instance, are only slightly larger than least weasels, and are common in much of Africa. They hunt small rodents in their underground burrows, and dig up lizards and insects. They are also very agile climbers, and sometimes hunt birds or steal their eggs.

Hunting in groups

Slender mongooses hunt alone, but other mongooses sometimes hunt in groups to catch particular kinds of prey, or at certain times of year. The narrow-banded mongoose, for instance, spends much of the year digging up grubs in the forests of Madagascar. However, in the wet season, groups of mongooses gather together to hunt mouse lemurs and chameleons through the trees.

Egyptian mongooses also sometimes hunt in groups. In Spain, they live in family groups and hunt rabbits. Rabbit warrens have many entrance holes, so when the mongooses go hunting each mongoose takes a different entrance.

The marsh mongoose is found close to rivers and swamps throughout Africa. This one is eating a young crocodile out of its egg.

Social mongooses

Some mongoose species eat mostly insects. Animals digging for insects have their heads down, and it is hard for them to spot approaching enemies. So insect-eating mongooses live together in large groups to share the work of watching out for danger.

Meerkats are social mongooses that live in dry regions in southern Africa. These mongooses dig for grubs and other insects during the day, then shelter in burrows at night. During the day, there are always one or two group members on sentry duty, keeping watch for danger. If they spot a predator, such as a jackal or an eagle, they make an alarm call, and everyone scampers for the safety of a burrow.

Not just insects

Meerkats eat mainly insects, but they do not pass up the chance of bigger prey. They often catch lizards and small snakes, and they also hunt scorpions. When a meerkat sniffs out a scorpion hiding under a stone, it flicks the stone off with its claws. The meerkat dodges the scorpion's pincers and bites at its body and even its stinging tail. Once the scorpion is dead, the meerkat eats it head-first.

A new generation

Solitary hunters, such as Indian Grey mongooses, have separate territories where they live and hunt. Males and females meet up only to **mate**, and the males do not help with bringing up the young.

Among social mongooses things are very different. Males and females live together in the same group. Each male or female has a rank in the

Meerkats occasionally get stung by scorpions, but they are hardly bothered by the sting, despite it being powerful enough to kill a rabbit.

Odd partners

Dwarf mongooses get unexpected help in watching out for danger when they are feeding. Hornbills are large birds that eat similar insect food to the mongooses. When the mongooses are hunting, they often disturb grasshoppers and flying insects, which the hornbills catch and eat. In return, the hornbills perch near to where the mongooses are feeding, and warn them if there are enemies in the area.

Dwarf mongooses often live in termite mounds (like this one). If they are late coming out to feed in the morning, their hornbill partners will give them a wake-up call.

group, and the top-ranked male and female mate and produce young more often than the others. Among dwarf mongooses, which are also social in their behaviour, only the top-ranking male and female mate.

Once the babies are born, the whole group helps to look after them. Adult males often bring the young food after they stop drinking mother's milk. "Babysitters" guard the young and keep them close to the burrow while the rest of the group feeds.

Babysitting is a real sacrifice for a meerkat. Adults need to eat most of the day in order to survive, and babysitters often have to go a whole day without food. This picture shows a mother, a babysitter and three baby kittens.

Fossa

In a forest in Madagascar, a fossa chases a **lemur**. In the trees the lemur holds its own, swinging through the branches at tremendous speed. But in some places there are clearings where the lemur has to come to the ground. It springs quickly across the forest floor, but the fossa is faster. With a burst of speed the fossa closes the gap, grapples the lemur to the ground and bites its throat.

Fossas look like small pumas, but in fact they belong to another group of Carnivores, the civets. Civets are small, cat-like animals that live in trees. Most are **omnivores**, but the fossa is a fierce predator that lives in the forests of Madagascar.

Hunting through the trees

Fossas are the biggest of the civets, measuring about 70 centimetres (27 inches) plus an equally long tail. Unlike cats and dogs, which walk on their toes, fossas walk on the whole foot like bears. They are tremendously agile climbers. They need all their agility to catch their favourite prey – lemurs.

Fossas usually hunt at night. They try to creep as close as possible to their prey before they attack. However they will also hunt lemurs by chasing them.

Fossas are usually red-brown in colour, although some are black. A fossa can leap from tree to tree, and run up a tree trunk like a squirrel.

Lemurs like this brown lemur (Lemur fulvus fulvus) are the fossa's main prey. Both the lemurs and the fossa are in danger of becoming extinct, because their forest home is being cut down.

Fossas also hunt birds and small mammals in the trees, and snakes and guinea fowl on the ground. As with their other prey, they rely on stealth to get close before making a final attack.

Mating and young

Fossas usually live alone, but in September and October females and males come together to **mate**. After mating they separate again, and the female raises the cubs alone.

The cubs are born about three months after mating, in a cave or other den. Fossa cubs develop slowly. Their eyes do not open until they are three weeks old, and they do not leave the den until they are about four months old. The young fossas stay with their mother for over a year, learning to hunt. After this they fend for themselves, but they are not ready to breed until they are about four years old.

Useful smells

Like the mustelids, most civets have a scent gland under the tail. This produces a thick, smelly substance called civet, which the animals use for scent-marking. Civet has been used for hundreds of years for making perfumes. In small amounts, it has a pleasant smell. More importantly, civet makes a perfume last longer, because it slows down the speed at which other smells in the perfume are released.

Spotted hyena

In the early evening, a group of female spotted hyenas leave their cubs and set out to hunt. The females have to travel 40 kilometres (25 miles) before they find a group of wildebeest. The hyenas single out a young wildebeest, and after a long chase they kill it. The hyenas eat as much as they can, then travel all the way back to their dens to feed their cubs.

Spotted hyenas are the largest of the hyenas, 125 to 145 centimetres from head to tail (50 to 57 inches). They live in Africa south of the Sahara desert. They are found in a range of habitats from deserts to forests, but not in rainforests.

People usually think of spotted hyenas as **scavengers**. Spotted hyenas do scavenge, but they do not get most of their food this way. In fact they are among Africa's top predators.

From rhinos to lizards

In most areas hyenas mainly hunt large prey, such as young wildebeest and gemsbok (a type of large antelope with long horns). Sometimes spotted hyenas catch prey as large as zebras. But they will hunt just about any animal, from a rhino calf to a lizard, if the opportunity arises.

Hyenas were once thought to be "cowardly" because they run at prey animals, then back away. What they are actually doing is challenging the prey and looking for weaknesses.

Bone crushers

Spotted hyenas have a crushing bite. Their strong teeth and jaws can crunch through bones, something that other predators, such as lions, cannot do. They also have very strong acid in their stomachs, which allows them to **digest** the **nutrients** in bones. This means that they can get more nutrients from their food than other predators.

Spotted hyenas generally hunt at night. They have an excellent sense of smell, and usually find prey by following their scent.

Tireless hunters

Lions and other big cats hunt by sneaking up on their prey and then pouncing, but spotted hyenas hunt differently. They begin a hunt by running through a herd of prey animals or charging at them, watching carefully to see what the animals do. They look for one animal that is in some way slower or weaker than the others. This is the animal they choose to attack.

The hyenas now begin to chase their chosen prey. Hyenas are fast runners, and they are tireless. They chase the animal until either it escapes, or it becomes exhausted and the hyenas can pull it down. Spotted hyenas are excellent hunters, but even so in seven hunts out of ten their prey escapes.

The leg bones of animals contain a rich, jelly-like marrow in the centre. Hyenas can crunch the bones to get at the marrow.

Hyena clans

Spotted hyenas live together in groups called clans. Each clan has a **territory** that it defends from its neighbours. Clans can range in size from five adults to as many as eighty.

An area rich in prey, such as the Ngorongoro Crater in east Africa, can support large clans living in small territories. In areas where there are few prey animals, such as the Kalahari Desert, clans are much smaller and they need much larger territories.

When hyenas meet after being apart for a time, they sniff and lick each other. These greeting ceremonies help to strengthen the bonds between clan members.

In hyena clans, the females are in charge. The dominant female is the clan leader. She decides where the clan will hunt, and where they will den. Each of the other females has a rank below the dominant female. The highest-ranking male in the clan is ranked below even the lowliest female. Males join in the hunting, but they are rarely allowed near the cubs' dens.

Rivals for food

Spotted hyenas and lions compete for very similar prey, and there is strong rivalry between them. Lions sometimes steal a hyena clan's kill, but a hyena clan sometimes steals food from a lioness or group of lionesses (they rarely chase away male lions).

Fighting from birth

In the **breeding season**, high-ranking male hyenas get to **mate** with female hyenas. About sixteen weeks after mating, one to three cubs are born. The cubs are kept safe in dens under the ground.

Spotted hyena cubs are unusual among carnivores, because they are born with their eyes open and a mostly full set of teeth.

Large groups of hyenas gather at a piece of **carrion**. With large numbers there is more chance of defending the food against lions.

Very soon after birth, cubs begin to fight to decide which one is dominant. The dominant cub gets the bigger share of the female's milk, and in some cases the weakest cub may die of starvation.

Because hyenas range over very large areas searching for food, the cubs remain in the dens, feeding on their mother's milk, until they are able to travel with the clan to kills. This takes about nine months.

By about eighteen months, young hyenas are hunting for themselves. Young females stay with their home clan, but young males leave and find themselves a place in another clan.

Laughs and whoops

A clan is a loose grouping, and hyenas within the clan are often widely spread within their territory. Members of the clan communicate and keep in touch using various calls. There are at least fourteen different calls, including a whooping cry that is used to call for reinforcements, and a laughing call that one hyena uses when it submits to another.

Hyena mothers leave their cubs for long periods to go hunting. While they are away the cubs stay in or very close to their dens.

Tasmanian devil

The quiet of the Tasmanian night is broken by a harsh, blood-curdling screech. There are more screeches, and a chorus of other sounds – grunts, howls, snorts, barks and horrible coughs. It sounds as if some terrible fight is taking place. Actually it is just a group of Tasmanian devils feeding.

Tasmanian devils are not members of the Carnivore order – they are the largest **marsupial** predators. Like other marsupials, they carry their young in pouches.

Tasmanian devils look like small, black bears, and are about the size of a small dog, 50 to 62 centimetres long (20 to 25 inches). They are found only on the Australian island of Tasmania. They live in a range of habitats, but they prefer dry forests of eucalyptus trees.

Scavengers and hunters

The Tasmanian devil has a reputation as a ferocious killer. It was given the name "devil" because of its fierce looks and the horrible noises it makes. Farmers killed devils because they thought the devils were killing and eating cattle and sheep.

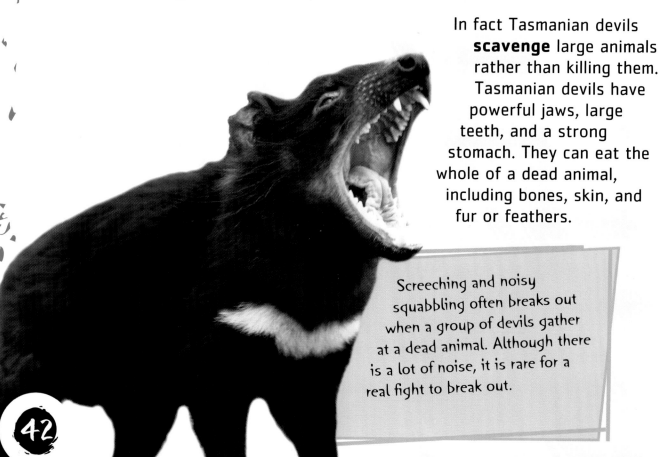

In fact Tasmanian devils **scavenge** large animals rather than killing them. Tasmanian devils have powerful jaws, large teeth, and a strong stomach. They can eat the whole of a dead animal, including bones, skin, and fur or feathers.

Screeching and noisy squabbling often breaks out when a group of devils gather at a dead animal. Although there is a lot of noise, it is rare for a real fight to break out.

As well as scavenging, devils also kill their own food. They hunt small mammals, birds, lizards, insects, and larger prey, such as wallabies. They kill with a bite to the head or chest.

Grains of rice

Tasmanian devils are active at night. During the day they rest in burrows, caves, or hollow logs. Devils live alone, but groups may meet up to feed on a dead animal.

In March, males and females pair up briefly and **mate**. The young are very tiny when they are born – little bigger than grains of rice. They crawl over the mother's fur and climb into a pouch on her belly. After about four months in the pouch, the pups emerge. They stay with their mother until the following February, when they become independent.

Thylacines

Until the 1930s, the world's largest marsupial predator was the thylacine or Tasmanian wolf. From the time European settlers arrived in the 1800s, thylacines were hunted because they had a reputation for killing sheep. Over-hunting, combined with a disease that killed many thylacines, led to them becoming extinct in 1936.

This picture of a captive thylacine is from 1930. Thylacines looked similar to dogs but had a pattern of stripes on their back. They probably fed on wallabies, possums, and birds.

Classification chart

Scientists classify living things (sort them into groups) by comparing their characteristics (their similarities and differences). A **species** is a group of animals or plants that are all similar and can breed together to produce young. Similar species are put together in a larger group called a **genus** (plural genera). Similar genera are grouped into **families**, and so on through bigger and bigger groupings – **classes**, **orders**, phyla, and kingdoms.

Carnivores (the order Carnivora) are mammals – they belong to the class Mammalia. The Tasmanian devil is not a Carnivore, but is a mammal. It belongs to the marsupial group (Marsupialia) and is part of the family Dasyuridae – the marsupial carnivores.

Order Carnivora

All families of the order are listed, but only examples that can be found in this book are listed.

Family	Number of genera	Number of species	Examples
Cat family (Felidae)	4	37	lions, tigers, leopards, cheetahs, domestic cats
Dog family (Canidae)	10	35	wolves, foxes, jackals, dingoes, wild and domestic dogs
Bears (Ursdiae)	3	8	polar bear, brown bear, spectacled bear, giant panda
Raccoons (Procyonidae)	7	19	raccoons, coatis, red panda
Weasel family (Mustelidae)	24	55	weasels, minks, polecats martens, sable, fisher, wolverine, otters, badgers
Skunks (Mephitidae)	3	10	skunks
Civets (Viverridae)	20	35	civets, genets, fossa
Mongooses (Herpestidae)	17	35	mongooses, meerkat
Hyenas (Hyaenidae)	4	4	hyenas, aardwolf

Where carnivores live

This map shows where some of the carnivores in this book live.

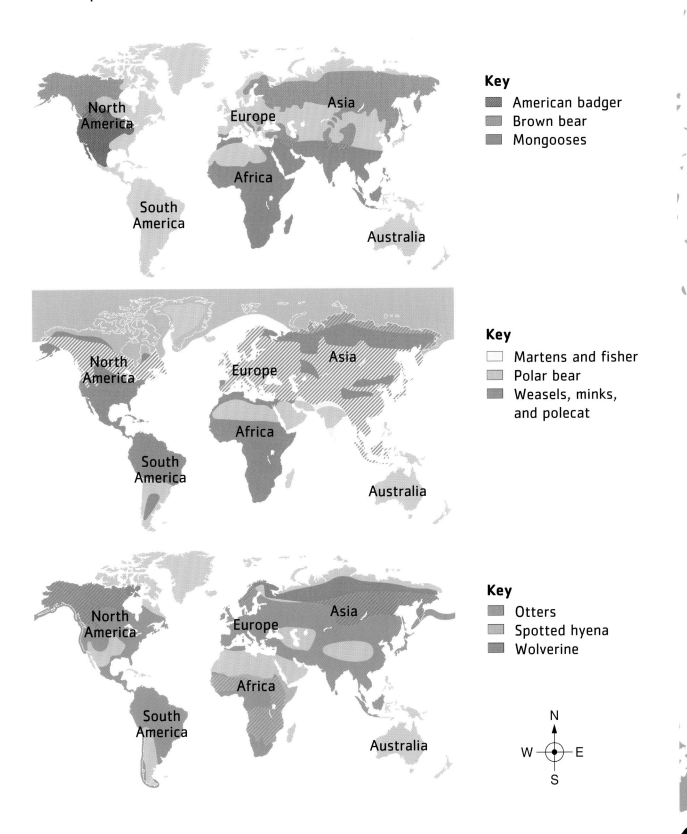

Key
- American badger
- Brown bear
- Mongooses

Key
- Martens and fisher
- Polar bear
- Weasels, minks, and polecat

Key
- Otters
- Spotted hyena
- Wolverine

Glossary

breeding season time of year when a group of animals mate

canines long, dagger-like teeth found in the mouth of most carnivores

carrion dead and rotting meat

class group of closely related families of living things

digest to break down food so that the body can extract nutrients from it

family group of closely related genera

fasting going without food

genus (plural genera) group of species of living things that are closely related

habitat place where an animal lives

hibernate to spend most of the winter in a deep sleep

insulator material that stops heat passing through it

lemurs agile, monkey-like animals found only in Madagascar. There are several species, most of which are similar in size to cats.

litter the young born to a female at one birth

mammals hairy, warm-blooded animals that feed their young on breast milk

marsupials group of mammals that give birth to very undeveloped young, which then live for a time in a pouch on their mother's stomach

mating when a male and a female animal come together to produce young

mustelids family of mammals that includes weasels, otters, mink, badgers, martens, and wolverines

nutrients substances in food that animals need to grow and get energy

omnivore animal that eats both animal and plant food

order group of closely related classes of living things

predator animal that hunts and eats other animals

prey animals that are hunted by predators

rodents family of mammals with sharp, gnawing front teeth that includes rats, mice, and squirrels

scavenge to eat scraps, or rubbish, or dead and rotting meat

scent marking marking a territory with urine or droppings

spawning when fish spawn the females lay eggs and the males fertilize them in the water

species group of animals that are similar and can breed together to produce healthy offspring

steppes large grassland areas in Russia and central Asia

territory area that an animal lives and hunts in, which it defends from other animals of the same species and sex

tundra cold, bleak lands around the Arctic

womb the place in a female mammal's body where her young develop

Further information

Books

African Predators, Martin Harvey and M. G. L. Mills (Smithsonian Books, November 2001)
Excellent section on hyenas, with wonderful photos.

Amazing Nature: Powerful Predators, Tim Knight (Heinemann Library, 2003)
A book exploring the amazing worlds of these fascinating animals.

The Velvet Claw: Natural History of the Carnivores, David W. Macdonald (BBC Consumer Books, 1992)
Full of fascinating information about Carnivores and their history.

Organizations and websites

www.enchantedlearning.com/subjects/mammals/weasel/Mustelids.shtml
Straightforward information and colouring pictures of several mustelids.

www.americazoo.com/goto/index/mammals/carnivora.htm
More about carnivores at America Zoo.

www.rudimentsofwisdom.com/themes/themes_animals.htm
This wonderful cartoon encyclopedia has articles on badgers and hyenas.

www.nationalgeographic.com/ottercam/
Movies of two otters, Splash and Slide, at National Geographic.

www.otter.org/
Skye Environmental Centre Ltd, Broadford, Isle of Skye IV49 9AQ. An organization dedicated to helping the world's otter species to survive.

Index

Titles in the *Wild Predators!* series include:

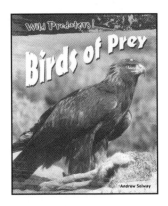

Hardback   0431189927

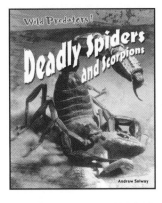

Hardback   0431189943

Hardback   0431190070

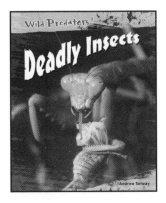

Hardback   0431190038

Hardback   0431190054

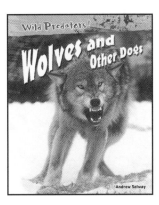

Hardback   0431189951

Hardback   0431190046

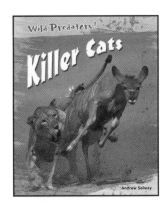

Hardback   0431190062

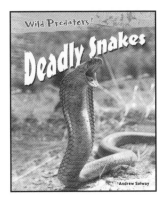

Hardback   0431189935

Hardback   0431189919

Find out about the other titles in this series on our website www.heinemann.co.uk/library